Why We Believe

Saralyn R. Bulovas

This book is a work of non-fiction. Unless otherwise noted, the author and the publisher make no explicit guarantees as to the accuracy of the information contained in this book and in some cases, names of people and places have been altered to protect their privacy.

WestBow Press books may be ordered through booksellers or by contacting:

WestBow Press
A Division of Thomas Nelson & Zondervan
1663 Liberty Drive
Bloomington, IN 47403
www.westbowpress.com
1 (866) 928-1240

ISBN: 978-1-4908-8911-5 (sc)
ISBN: 978-1-4908-8910-8 (e)

Library of Congress Control Number: 2015910771

Print information available on the last page.

WestBow Press rev. date: 07/16/2015

WESTBOW PRESS
A DIVISION OF THOMAS NELSON & ZONDERVAN

T'was the night before Christmas and we were decorating the tree.

Listening to the story that tells why we believe.

Upon a donkey, Mary did ride.

She traveled to Bethlehem with Joseph by her side.

A humble stable is where they were led.

The manger filled with hay was used as a bed.

Baby Jesus was born on this most Holy night.

He was sent from Heaven to bring goodness and light.

Angels proclaimed His birth with glee.

Shepherds adored Him on bended knee.

A bright star showed Three Wise Men the way.

They placed their gifts beside the baby asleep on the hay.

Jesus is the reason!

We celebrate each Christmas season.

The nativity reminds us of our dear Savior's birth.

Wishing you love, joy and peace on earth.

Luke 1:14

You will have joy and gladness, and many will rejoice at his birth.

Lightning Source UK Ltd.
Milton Keynes UK
UKHW050933060519
342171UK00006B/89/P

9 781490 889115